QL
665
.F57
Cop.1

Fisher, Don

Reptiles, past and present

DATE DUE

REF
QL-665
.F57
Cop.1

FORM 125 M

Business/Science/Technology
Division

The Chicago Public Library

MAR 23 1978

Received

# REPTILES
# PAST AND PRESENT

REPTILES PAST AND PRESENT
WRITTEN AND ILLUSTRATED BY DON FISHER

*Publishers*
T. S. DENISON & COMPANY, INC.
*Minneapolis, Minnesota*

 T. S. DENISON & COMPANY, INC.

All rights reserved, including the right to reproduce this book, or portions thereof, except that permission is hereby granted to reviewers to quote brief passages in a review to be printed in magazines and newspapers, or for radio and television reviews.

Standard Book Number: 513-01513-2
Printed in the United States of America
by The Brings Press
Copyright © 1976 by T. S. Denison & Co., Inc.
Minneapolis, Minn. 55437

# CONTENTS

INTRODUCTION. . . . . . . . . . . 3
1. DINOSAURS. . . . . . . . . . . . . . 4
2. SNAKES. . . . . . . . . . . . . . . . 19
3. LIZARDS. . . . . . . . . . . . . . . 29
4. CROCODILIA. . . . . . . . . . . . 41
5. TURTLES. . . . . . . . . . . . . . . 49

## INTRODUCTION

The long extinct dinosaurs have brought about a great interest in reptiles. They are as interesting as the dinosaurs who ruled the world for millions of years. Reptiles are linked to the past and we learn about life that existed millions of years ago through the study of them.

# SEYMOURIA

Three hundred million years ago this small (less than six feet long) lizard roamed the carboniferous swamps and forests of the world. Seymouria, unlike his water-dwelling ancestors, had claws and lungs and no longer was dependent on oceans and rivers for existence. Although very slow and clumsy this species lived nearly 130 million years before dying out. Today's reptiles, as well as some dinosaurs, can be traced directly back to him.

# SEYMOURIA

# BRONTOSAURUS

The Brontosaurus was one of the largest animals that ever walked on earth. His living weight may have exceeded thirty-five tons and they often grew to a length of eighty feet. He is exceeded in size only by the greatest of modern whales. The Brontosaurus spent most of his life in the water. It helped support his great bulk. Brontosaurus was a vegetarian, eating aquatic plants which grew in abundance, and tree tops. Fossil remains of the Brontosaurus are found in the western United States.

# BRONTOSAURUS

# TRICERATOPS
# (TRY-CER-A-TOPS)

    Triceratops means "three-horned face". Two gigantic horns stuck out from his huge head, while the third horn was on his nose. He had a thick squat body nearly thirty feet long while his skull was about ten feet long. It is thought that all dinosaurs feared the Triceratops because of his great strength and terrible horns. He was a strict vegetarian. Triceratops lived on land and spent most of his time in marsh grasses east of the Rocky Mountains.

# TRICERATOPS

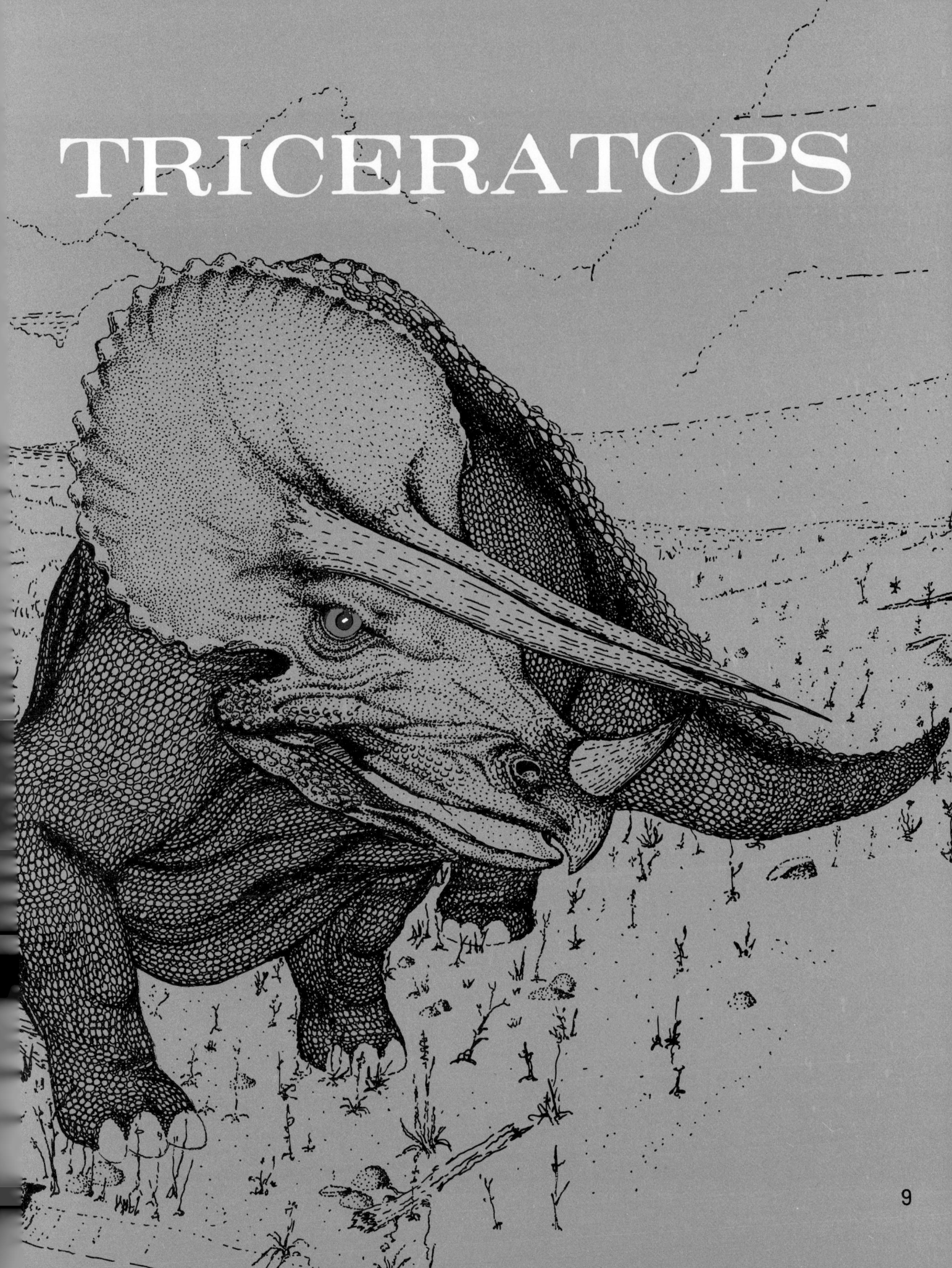

# TYRANNOSAURUS REX (KING OF TYRANTS)

The most fearsome creature that ever walked the earth. Nothing was safe from this monster unless it lived in the sea. Tyrannosaurus was a very fast dinosaur because of his well-developed powerful hind legs and tail. His short forelimbs were tiny, but his claws were like spring steel. His body was as long as a freight car. His head was enormous with jaws four feet long with six-inch, long dagger-like teeth and he weighed nearly eight tons. A flesh-eating creature, Tyrannosaurus would eat anything he could catch and he could catch most anything.

Many fossilized skeletons of this tyrant have been found in the Dakotas and Montana.

# TYRANNOSAURUS REX

11

# ANATOSAUR

This peaceful fairly large duck-billed dinosaur lived in North America. Several skeletons including many well-preserved skins or mummies have been found. Anatosaurs, unlike the Tyrannosaurus, developed a spine that would allow him to walk upright as pictured or on all four legs to seek out fresh-water plants. These plants were shoveled out with their well-developed duckbills. The Anatosaurus skull contained more than 2000 flat, grinding, closely-packed teeth.

ANATOSAUR

# PLESIOSAURUS

This 40-foot-long sea serpent never came out on land. They lived like turtles rather than fish but did not have a shell. His neck was long, his head was small and contained many needle-sharp teeth. He could catch his prey with a quick movement, using his long neck to reach out. They were capable of moving backward as well as forward.

Plesiosaurus' life-line began more than 150 million years ago and lasted about seventy million years before dying out, leaving no traceable descendents.

# PLESIOSARUS

# PTERANODON

Seventy-five million years ago the Cretaceous skies were dark with very large ugly flying Pteranodons. The Pteranodon was not a bird but a flying reptile. He could not take off as a bird does, but had to leap from a high place such as a cliff and seek upward currents of air to stay aloft, somewhat like today's large gliding birds. Unlike birds they had no feathers, only skin stretched over an extended hollow arm and finger bones. Their wing-spread sometimes reached a length of twenty-seven feet. After leaving their nest on high ocean cliffs the female only returned to these cliffs to lay eggs and then returned to the ocean skies leaving the eggs unguarded to hatch in the sun.

Pteranodon died out seventy million years ago, leaving no descendants.

# PTERANODON

# THE TIME OF GREAT DYING

About sixty-three million years ago the great dinosaur era came to a close. The exact reason for this is not known. Climate changes played a large part in their extinction. The dinosaurs were cold-blooded reptiles and could not survive in the Ice Age that was upon them. If large dinosaurs such as the Brontosaurus could have survived the cold, the vegetation they fed upon could not have. Some scientists think they became too specialized, while others feel smaller animals ate their eggs. Another reason might have been their lack of intelligence as compared to the large meat eating mammals that preyed upon them.

Only five orders of reptiles survived "the time of great dying".

Of these orders there are about 6000 different kinds: 200 turtles, 23 crocodiles and alligators, 1 tuatara, 2700 snakes and 3000 lizards.

# SNAKES

Our world today has more than 2700 different kinds of snakes. They range in size from the five inches of a small burrowing snake all the way to the 35-foot python. Some snakes are deadly poison. But most are not. In fact, there are some snakes like the Rosy Boa that make no attempt to bite. Some snakes will attack man when angered or frightened, but so will any animal even the timid mouse.

Snakes differ greatly in the way they catch their food. Some, like the Boa Constrictor, squeeze their victim until it suffocates. Some use poison to kill their victim while others catch and swallow their food alive. Most snakes lay eggs but some give birth to live babies. These baby snakes must find their own food from the day they are born, because the mother snake like all reptiles will not feed her young and in most cases is gone before they hatch. Some snakes grow large enough to capture and swallow an animal as large as a deer.

# RATTLESNAKE

The Rattlesnake is one of America's most deadly and dangerous snakes. They are very poisonous even from birth and must be avoided. Some Rattlesnakes grow to a length of nine feet. Rattlers are important because their main diet consists of rodent pests and control their spread to some extent.

The Rattlesnake's name comes from the rattle on the end of its body. Each time the snake sheds its skin it adds a hollow boney segment to its tail. These loosely joined segments give a loud rattle when the snake is startled or in danger.

The venom (poison) of the Rattlesnake as well as some other poisonous snakes is valuable in certain medicines and as an antidote in some snake bite cases.

Rattlesnakes are all poisonous and should not be kept as a pet, even if defanged (long injector teeth removed) as they will grow new ones.

# RATTLESNAKE

# KING SNAKE

King Snakes are among the most beautiful snakes in America. When fully grown they range in length from eighteen inches to five feet.

King Snakes are beneficial because of the large amount of rodents and poisonous snakes they consume. The King Snake is one of the few animals that seem to be immune to the venom of the Rattlesnake and include rattlers in their diet.

The King Snake may strike, but not bite when captured. It will soon tame down and make a beautiful pet if properly cared for. In captivity they eat mice, sparrows and smaller snakes. A large King Snake measures about five feet. They lay from ten to fourteen eggs. They hatch in five to six weeks.

# KING SNAKE

# COPPERHEAD

    Copperheads are the most common poisonous snakes found in the Eastern United States. This medium-sized, copper-colored snake is a very poisonous relative of the Rattlesnake. Copperheads, like the rattlers, are known as Pit Vipers because of deep pits between their eyes. They are sensitive to heat, helping them locate warm-blooded animals such as rodents and assuring them an accurate strike. A quiet snake, the Copperhead will fight when stepped on or disturbed. It prefers to take refuge in crevices among rocks. In winter it goes into a crevice to hibernate. The female gives birth to living young. These young snakelets possess enough venom to kill a mouse. The young have bright yellow tails that turn to brown by the third year. Within ten days after birth the young shed their skin for the first time. The chief enemies of the Copperhead, besides man, are other snakes, especially the King Snake.

# COPPERHEAD

# BOA CONSTRICTOR

Some Boas are among the world's most beautiful snakes. They range in length from less than four feet to thirty feet.

The Boa Constrictor is one of several Boas. There are records of eighteen foot Boa Constrictors. They are non-poisonous and kill their prey by coiling its body around the victim. Then the reptile begins to squeeze, cutting off breathing and circulation.

The United States has two Boas, the Rosy Boa and the Rubber Boa. The Rubber Boa is not a beautiful snake as far as markings and color is concerned. They are rather plain brown with faint or no markings. On the other hand, the Rosy Boa is a very beautiful snake, having three distinct black strips running the entire length of its ivory-colored body, one on top and one on each side as pictured. Boa Constrictors can be easily tamed and make an interesting and educational reptile pet. Some Boas have endured zoo life for more than twenty years. The Boa is active in early hours and this is when feeding takes place.

# BOA CONSTRICTOR

# LIZARDS

There are more than 3000 different kinds of lizards living today. They range in size from the two inches of the Tiny Fence Lizard to the twelve foot Komodo "Dragon" Lizard. Although closely related, snakes and lizards differ greatly. Most lizards have four legs, eye lids that close, scales that go all around their body, and are able to hear air-born sounds with their external ears.

Lizards are found the world over, except in very cold areas. Most are land lizards but some are capable of swimming. Lizards differ in another respect to snakes: They do not have poisonous fangs to help catch food. But they do have long sticky tongues and an accurate aim for catching insects. Some eat eggs of birds and other reptiles, some are entirely vegetarian. Some swallow their food whole.

# AMERICAN CHAMELEON (ANOLE)

    The Anole is very common in the Southeastern United States. They are attractive and have the ability to change color to match their surroundings, this color change comes through various causes: sun, temperature, sickness or anger. The Anole moves sly like a cat. It hides among dense treetops and when an insect is spotted its long sticky tongue darts out with deadly accuracy and snaps its victim back into its mouth. The males fight furiously with each other.

    Although thousands of Anoles are sold through pet stores, they do not live beyond a few months because their appetite decreases and they soon stop eating.

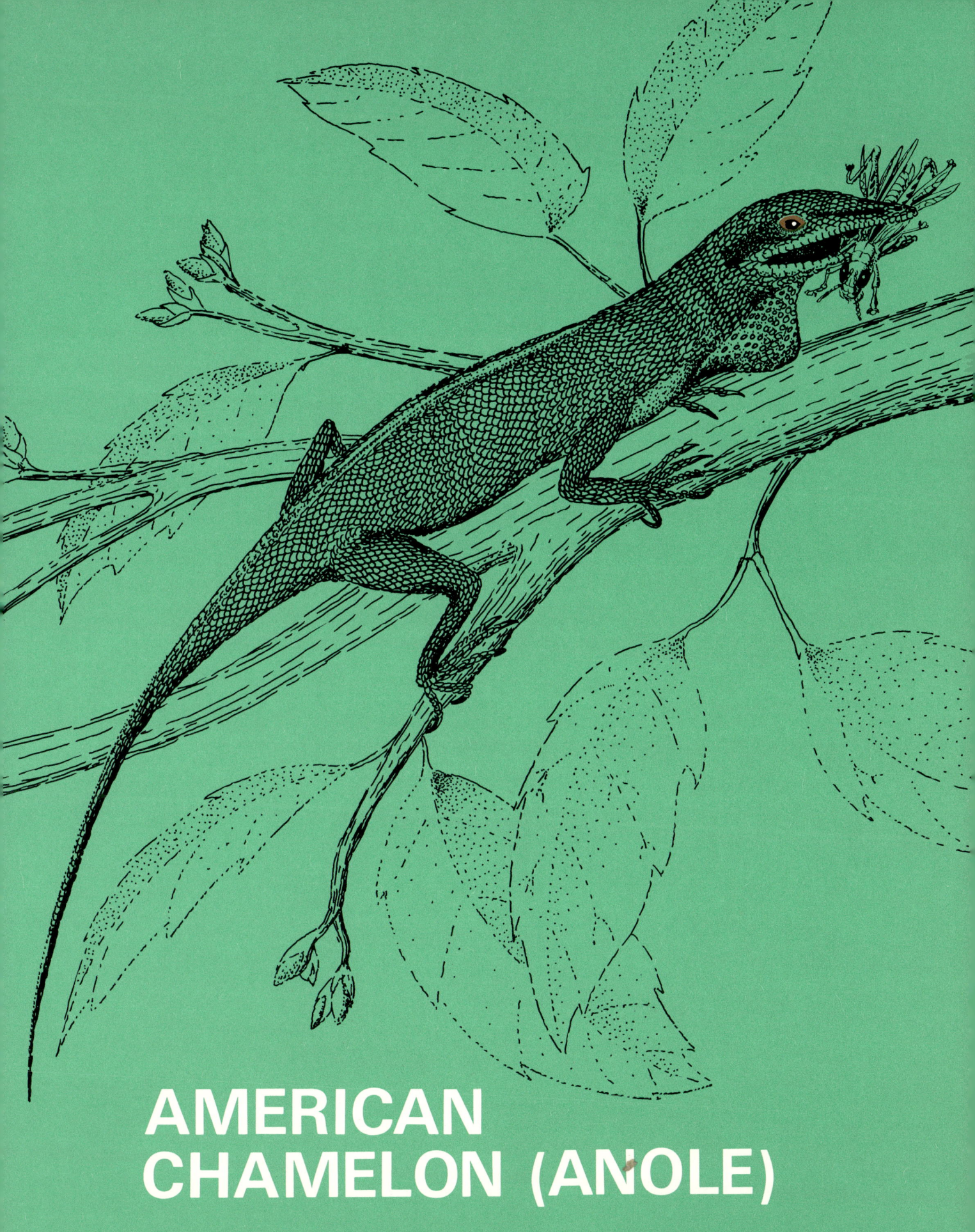

# AMERICAN CHAMELON (ANOLE)

# GILA MONSTER

Gila, pronounced Hela, Monsters are found in the Southwestern Desert Region of the United States and Mexico. The Gila Monster is America's only poisonous lizard, but it does not bite and inject poison as a snake does because it doesn't have fangs (injector teeth). When the lizard bites, poison flows into the wound from its salivary glands. Gilas are slow-moving, clumsy reptiles but when threatened or captured can bite swiftly and hang on strongly.

The Gila Monster may grow to a length of two feet. It feeds on toads, lizards and insects as well as eggs of snakes and lizards, which it digs out of the sand. When food is plentiful the tail fills out, and when it's not available, it absorbs the fat stored in the tail.

# GILA MONSTER

# HORNED LIZARD

This interesting little creature (sometimes referred to as the "Horned Toad") is found in the deserts of Central and Southern United States. They are harmless to man. Usually slow moving they are capable of swift movement. The Horned Toad is unique because when frightened or angry it squirts a thin stream of blood from the corners of its eyes. The Horned Lizard has a broad body like a toad. Their color makes good protection in the desert.

This little lizard, sometimes seven inches long, is often captured by tourists. However, they will usually die due to lack of sun, improper food, cold or dampness. Horned Toads like to hibernate. If unable to, they usually survive the winter only to die in the spring.

# HORNED TOAD

# MARINE IGUANA

This large (five feet long) lizard is a very skillful swimmer. They fear only a shark while in the seas and possess no enemies on land.

The Marine Iguana feeds on seaweed and ocean algae. They are found on the volcanic island of Galapagos and is one of the very few lizards that swim. They have webbed feet and very long sharp claws to help them climb the volcanic rocks of their island. They are capable of holding onto a rock amid a strong surf. During the daytime hours the rocks are literally covered with thousands of dark blue-green and orange fierce-looking monsters sunning themselves. Although fierce looking they are quite lazy and tame, they have never been known to attack a man, even when teased. They are able to walk on the ocean bottom. At night they dig burrows in soft lava above the shore line and when in these burrows it is difficult to pull them to the surface, due to the strength of their claws. The Marine Iguana is the only animal that can control its heart beat when under water and even stop it if necessary.

# MARINE IGUANA

# KOMODO DRAGON (LIZARD)

The Komodo Dragon is the largest living lizard. When fully grown they may weigh 300 pounds or more and grow to a length of twelve feet.

The Komodo Dragon is named for the Pacific Island they were discovered on in 1912. Due to game preserves by the Dutch Government the dragons are fairly numerous now. This monster lizard feeds on flesh of living creatures or the decayed meat of dead animals. If hungry enough they will run down their prey, which includes wild pigs, deer, goats and sometimes man. Like all lizards they do not chew their food, but bolt it down intact, bones, fur and all. If the prey is too large to swallow, they tear it into smaller pieces. When they have eaten their fill the Komodo Lizard becomes extremely lazy. In captivity they become quite docile.

# KOMODO DRAGON

# CROCODILIANS

Tropical and sub-tropical countries claim one or more species of Crocodilians, Crocodiles, Alligators and Gavials. These are the largest of modern reptiles and are the last surviving descendants of the stock that produced the great dinosaurs. Crocodilians are strong swimmers. They can dive and reappear under their victim. Crocodilians, as a rule, are not aggressive animals and will run away rather than fight a man. But there are some man-eating Crocodilia that exist, and hunger will drive them to the kill. Full grown they range in size from three feet to twenty-three feet. Some Crocodilians have been known to live to fifty years of age.

# AMERICAN ALLIGATOR

Except for size the American Alligator has remained unchanged for millions of years. This mild-mannered reptile is not usually dangerous but will defend itself with great vigor if cornered. The adult alligator may grow to a length of ten to fifteen feet and weigh several hundred pounds and is among the best swimming animals. Full adulthood comes about the ninth year. It is at this time that the female begins to lay eggs. Breeding comes in early spring once the eggs are laid. The mother spends all her time near the nest to protect them. Laws now protect the alligator, but they still face the possibility of extinction. The sale of baby alligators is now prohibited.

# AMERICAN ALLIGATOR

# SOUTH AMERICAN CAIMAN

The South American Caiman is a close relative of the more mild-mannered American Alligator but are somewhat smaller. The average adult Caiman may reach a length of six to twelve feet long. The Caiman is the noisiest member of the crocodilia family with sounds ranging from growls and croaks to snorts and hisses. He is a fierce biter. Baby Caimans (pictured) are sold as alligators through pet stores but do not make good pets because of their bad temper. Even a new-born Caiman will display his needle-sharp teeth, thrash violently and bite viciously. They are also very hard to feed.

# SOUTH AMERICAN CAIMAN

# CROCODILE

The Crocodile like the American Alligator has remained basically unchanged for the last sixty million years. It is of the same breed that long ago produced the great dinosaurs. The Crocodile is one of the largest members of the Crocodilia family, growing to a length of nearly twenty feet. The adult feeds on mammals, fish and reptiles (sometimes its own young). Some Crocodiles are man-eaters. Fortunately very few Crocodiles live in the United States. Some Crocodiles like salt water and often swim far out to sea in search of large fish to feed upon. Some prefer salt marshes for breeding and nesting. The Crocodile like the Caiman has a very bad temper.

# CROCODILE

## TURTLES

Turtles ancestors first appeared some two hundred million years ago, long before the great dinosaurs, and have remained relatively unchanged for some one hundred fifty million years. The exact reason the Turtle survived the time of great dying is not known. But part of the reason for this long survival may be their unusual skeleton. The top shell or carapace is actually overgrown widened ribs. Another, some have the ability to withdraw into their shell for protection, ability to remain submerged for long periods of time and eat almost anything from leaves to lizards. Turtles unlike the most of the great dinosaurs are able to live most anywhere, in deserts, swamps or open seas. This great flexibility must have contributed heavily to their survival.

# BOX TURTLE

The United States has two kinds of Box Turtles, the Eastern Box Turtle and the Western Box Turtle. These two differ slightly in markings but are the same otherwise. Both feed on insects, worms, fruit and vegetables. Being polite they accept all food offered and may put on excess weight. Like most land turtles the Box Turtle can withdraw completely into his shell when frightened or threatened. Inside he is safe from most predators. Those in captivity may not attempt to close their shell. These friendly turtles make very good trouble-free pets as they do not bite. They need not be caged when inside the home as they are very clean; but they should be penned up for feeding. In captivity they eat worms, lettuce, raw meat and fruit. Our turtle is no problem to find as he follows the same path through the house and is usually at the same place at the same time each day. In captivity the Box Turtle is a very pleasant and clever creature.

Box Turtles are fully grown at twenty years and may live as long as eighty years.

# BOX TURTLE

# SNAPPING TURTLE

Snapping Turtles are among the largest inland turtles in the United States. They live in fresh water lakes, creeks and rivers. Snappers sometimes attain a length of two feet and weigh nearly sixty pounds.

They feed on fresh-water animals, marsh grass and vegetables. However, the Snapper can go for months with no food. Their shell is small and they cannot withdraw all of their legs and head, but because of their size and strength have little need to hide.

Snapping Turtles, because of their size and appetite, sometimes eat all of the fish off an unsuspecting fisherman's stringer or strip the bait off his hooks. Snappers live to be quite old, some zoos reported to have in captivity Snapping Turtles aged to sixty years. Snapping Turtles have a terrible temper and are one of the most dangerous turtles and have been known to crush a man's arm with their powerful beak. Young turtles are on their own from birth as the mother offers no help or training. Thé Snapper is drawn to the aquatic life the instant it's born.

# SNAPPING TURTLE

# SOFT-SHELLED TURTLE

Soft-Shell Turtles have, in fact, hard or tough leathery shells but the edges are soft and pliable and the top of the shell is smooth, lacking the rough plates of other turtles. Their long beak serves as a snorkle so they can remain submerged and still breath. In time of danger the feet and slender head can be withdrawn into the shell. This rather large turtle, attaining a length of eighteen inches and weighing nearly forty pounds is found in streams, lake and river beds throughout most of America. These turtles feed on shellfish, fish and frogs. The Soft-Shelled Turtle like the Snapper has a snakelike neck capable of darting after prey. Their claws and sharp beak are used in hunting their food. They are noted for their bad temper.

# SOFT SHELLED TURTLE

# GREEN SEA TURTLE

This graceful, fast-swimming Sea Turtle has direct ancestors dating back as far as a hundred million years. They were at one time, land turtles, but due to possible climate changes and lack of food took refuge in the oceans. Over millions of years they have developed efficient swim fins and flattened shells that help them swim well. In fact, in the water they are among the fastest-moving reptiles. This beautiful turtle swims thousands of miles a year and only the female returns to land to lay eggs. She may lay two hundred to five hundred flexible white eggs in a large hole. She digs with her hind legs, smooths out the sand over the eggs and then returns to the sea. Soon the eggs hatch and the beach is covered with thousands of young. Only a few of the young reach adulthood. Sea birds eat many of them, and most of those that do reach the sea are eaten by fish. Adult Sea Turtles may weigh from seventy-five to one hundred fifty pounds, and have a length of nearly six feet. If recent conservation attempts fail, this harmless reptile along with many other animals will vanish into the history books, because of a few selfish human beings.

# GREEN SEA TURTLE

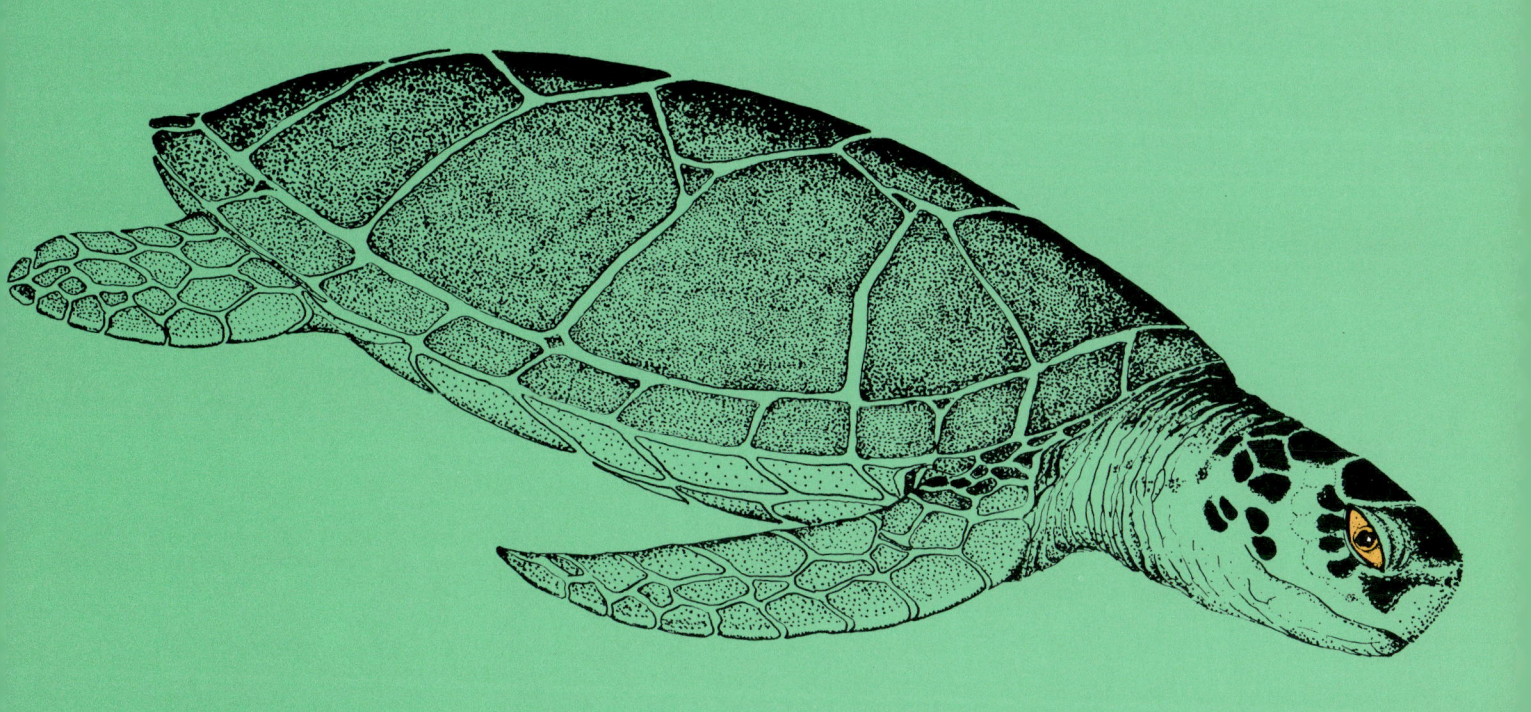

## INDEX

Seymouria . . . . . . . . . . . . . . . . . . . . . . . . . . . . . . . . . 4
Brontosaurus . . . . . . . . . . . . . . . . . . . . . . . . . . . . . . 6
Triceratops . . . . . . . . . . . . . . . . . . . . . . . . . . . . . . . . 8
Tyrannosaurus Rex . . . . . . . . . . . . . . . . . . . . . . . . 10
Anatosaur . . . . . . . . . . . . . . . . . . . . . . . . . . . . . . . . 12
Plesiosarus . . . . . . . . . . . . . . . . . . . . . . . . . . . . . . . 14
Pteranodon . . . . . . . . . . . . . . . . . . . . . . . . . . . . . . . 16
Rattlesnake . . . . . . . . . . . . . . . . . . . . . . . . . . . . . . . 20
King Snake . . . . . . . . . . . . . . . . . . . . . . . . . . . . . . . 22
Copperhead . . . . . . . . . . . . . . . . . . . . . . . . . . . . . . 24
Boa Constrictor . . . . . . . . . . . . . . . . . . . . . . . . . . . 26
American Chameleon . . . . . . . . . . . . . . . . . . . . . 31
Gila Monster . . . . . . . . . . . . . . . . . . . . . . . . . . . . . 33
Horned Toad . . . . . . . . . . . . . . . . . . . . . . . . . . . . . 35
Marine Iguana . . . . . . . . . . . . . . . . . . . . . . . . . . . 37
Komodo Dragon . . . . . . . . . . . . . . . . . . . . . . . . . 39
American Alligator . . . . . . . . . . . . . . . . . . . . . . . 43
South American Caiman . . . . . . . . . . . . . . . . . . 45
Crocodile . . . . . . . . . . . . . . . . . . . . . . . . . . . . . . . . 47
Box Turtle . . . . . . . . . . . . . . . . . . . . . . . . . . . . . . . 51
Snapping Turtle . . . . . . . . . . . . . . . . . . . . . . . . . . 53
Soft Shelled Turtle . . . . . . . . . . . . . . . . . . . . . . . . 55
Green Sea Turtle . . . . . . . . . . . . . . . . . . . . . . . . . 57